The
P@$$WORD
Log

An Internet Password Book

With tips for keeping your
information secure

Keeping your information safe in the age of identity theft is difficult enough but trying to keep track of all of your usernames, passwords, security questions, and more is almost impossible!

Keeping a log of all of these passwords is prudent. Saving them in your phone or on your computer is great until it crashes. Sticky notes get unstuck or lost and then you have to jump through hoop after hoop to reset your password. This book will keep all of that vital information in one easy to find place.

Worried about people snooping through your log? We have included tips to keep the nosy busybodies at bay. We also have tips for creating safe, secure passwords that will stop hackers dead in their tracks!

Did you know the most commonly used passwords are "password" and "123456"?

Easy to remember, sure. Easy to hack, absolutely.

Here are ways to create safer, more secure passwords!

Top Tips for Making Your Accounts Hard to Hack

1. **Make your password long.** It takes less than a second to hack a short password. By adding more characters, letters, and numbers you add to a hacker's frustration. While an 8-digit password takes 5 hours to crack, an 11-digit password takes 10 years to crack. Go to 12—

digits and the hacker's great-great grandchildren still won't have cracked the code!

2. **Include Uppercase, Lowercase, Numbers and Symbols.** "Password" takes only a second to crack, but "P@s$w0rD" takes 14 years. Use these special characters along with numbers and upper- and lower-case letters to make your password more impenetrable.

3. **Make your password nonsensical.** It's easier to crack the code if it's a common word or phrase. If possible, just jumble up a random mix, like your keyboard is confused "$Gdle863n*dnszM2" If it's too hard to make up a

nonsense password, try combining words with no connection, like your favorite ice cream flavor with your favorite car and a special year. Then mix in those special characters and cases. So, your new password might be "RuMrai$inD3lore@n1919". Good luck hacking that one!

4. **Don't use personal information that is easy to obtain**. Maybe you think your dog's name, Mr. Fluffypants, isn't something everyone knows. But if you posted a cute story about him on Facebook or tweeted about him #mrfluffypants or put that cute pic of him in a hat on Instagram, chances are his name isn't all that

unfamiliar. Your birthday, anniversary, high school, mother's maiden name, where you were born – all of these things are easy to find out on the Internet and social media. And stop taking and posting all of those "quizzes" that get you to reveal all kinds of personal information. You may not think that announcing your favorite sports team is going to give hackers any advantage, but if your password is Soxfan72 you might as well hand the hackers your money now.

5. **Don't use just one password.** Sure, it's easy to remember that your password for every site is "Myp@s$word84" but if hackers get it off of one

innocuous site, they can try it on other sites, like your bank, credit card company, etc. By having different passwords for different sites, hackers don't get a free pass to all of your information. And since you have this logbook, it won't matter that you have a hundred passwords since you are keeping them all organized.

6. **Change your passwords regularly**. Sites get hacked all of the time, so changing your password regularly just makes sense. The more sensitive your information is, the more often you should change them. Any site with financial information or identity information should

be changed the most frequently. And if you receive notice that a site you used has been compromised, change your password immediately, even if your information wasn't accessed. And don't reuse the same password again for a very, very long time.

7. **When answering security questions, lie.** Sure, it's easy to remember the answer to the security question "What's your dog's name?" but as we already established it's also pretty easy for strangers to obtain that information. But not if you lie. So, tell them your dog's name is Philodendron or Cell Phone Strap. No one is checking for accuracy.

Write down your answers though because if you don't remember your lie, the security questions become moot.

8. **Don't share your passwords.** You might share your Netflix password with Joe because he's your bud, but he might not be as careful as you are in sharing information. And remember, have different passwords for every site so if you do decide to share your Netflix, they can't access your Hulu too!

How to Keep This Logbook Spy Safe

After we spend all that time creating safer, more secure passwords and logins, what happens if someone finds this book? Well, here are some tips for making even this book harder to hack!

1. **Change it around.** Write your passwords down but write them backwards. You will know that they are backwards, but the person snooping your details won't. Or add a number, letter, character to your written password that isn't in the real password.

You know there is no Z in your passwords but Nosy McNoserson doesn't.

2. **Consider writing hints instead of the actual password.** Say your password is the phrase "Where'$theB33f?" – just write Wendy's commercial in the password line. For your security question answers (which are lies, remember?) instead of writing "Philodendron" under Security question 1, write "houseplant" or some other phrase to remind you of the answer.

3. **Don't leave the logbook out in the open.** Hide it amongst other books or papers. Post it notes stuck to your laptop are an

invitation to snoopers. By putting your password log someplace out of sight, your would be snoopster will be thwarted.

4. **Change the website name.** Instead of listing your Amazon password under the name Amazon, call it something else, like Car Parts. You will know what it means but others won't.

5. **Make your password an acronym for something.** Try making your password an acronym for a phrase by using just the first letter of each word in the phrase like "IE1−2coow$eM" but in your password line write "I eat ½ cup of oatmeal with strawberries every morning". You will know

what that means but no one
else will.

WEBSITE: _____

USER NAME: _____

PASSWORD: _____

SECURITY ANSWER 1: _____

SECURITY ANSWER 2: _____

SECURITY ANSWER 3: _____

ADDITIONAL INFO: _____

_____

****

WEBSITE: _____

USER NAME: _____

PASSWORD: _____

SECURITY ANSWER 1: _____

SECURITY ANSWER 2: _____

SECURITY ANSWER 3: _____

ADDITIONAL INFO: _____

_____

WEBSITE: _____

USER NAME: _____

PASSWORD: _____

SECURITY ANSWER 1: _____

SECURITY ANSWER 2: _____

SECURITY ANSWER 3: _____

ADDITIONAL INFO: _____

_____

****

WEBSITE: _____

USER NAME: _____

PASSWORD: _____

SECURITY ANSWER 1: _____

SECURITY ANSWER 2: _____

SECURITY ANSWER 3: _____

ADDITIONAL INFO: _____

_____

WEBSITE: _____

USER NAME: _____

PASSWORD: _____

SECURITY ANSWER 1: _____

SECURITY ANSWER 2: _____

SECURITY ANSWER 3: _____

ADDITIONAL INFO: _____

_____

****

WEBSITE: _____

USER NAME: _____

PASSWORD: _____

SECURITY ANSWER 1: _____

SECURITY ANSWER 2: _____

SECURITY ANSWER 3: _____

ADDITIONAL INFO: _____

_____

WEBSITE: _____

USER NAME: _____

PASSWORD: _____

SECURITY ANSWER 1: _____

SECURITY ANSWER 2: _____

SECURITY ANSWER 3: _____

ADDITIONAL INFO: _____

_____

****

WEBSITE: _____

USER NAME: _____

PASSWORD: _____

SECURITY ANSWER 1: _____

SECURITY ANSWER 2: _____

SECURITY ANSWER 3: _____

ADDITIONAL INFO: _____

_____

WEBSITE: _____

USER NAME: _____

PASSWORD: _____

SECURITY ANSWER 1: _____

SECURITY ANSWER 2: _____

SECURITY ANSWER 3: _____

ADDITIONAL INFO: _____

_____

****

WEBSITE: _____

USER NAME: _____

PASSWORD: _____

SECURITY ANSWER 1: _____

SECURITY ANSWER 2: _____

SECURITY ANSWER 3: _____

ADDITIONAL INFO: _____

_____

WEBSITE: _____

USER NAME: _____

PASSWORD: _____

SECURITY ANSWER 1: _____

SECURITY ANSWER 2: _____

SECURITY ANSWER 3: _____

ADDITIONAL INFO: _____

_____

****

WEBSITE: _____

USER NAME: _____

PASSWORD: _____

SECURITY ANSWER 1: _____

SECURITY ANSWER 2: _____

SECURITY ANSWER 3: _____

ADDITIONAL INFO: _____

_____

WEBSITE: _____

USER NAME: _____

PASSWORD: _____

SECURITY ANSWER 1: _____

SECURITY ANSWER 2: _____

SECURITY ANSWER 3: _____

ADDITIONAL INFO: _____

_____

****

WEBSITE: _____

USER NAME: _____

PASSWORD: _____

SECURITY ANSWER 1: _____

SECURITY ANSWER 2: _____

SECURITY ANSWER 3: _____

ADDITIONAL INFO: _____

_____

WEBSITE: _____

USER NAME: _____

PASSWORD: _____

SECURITY ANSWER 1: _____

SECURITY ANSWER 2: _____

SECURITY ANSWER 3: _____

ADDITIONAL INFO: _____

_____

****

WEBSITE: _____

USER NAME: _____

PASSWORD: _____

SECURITY ANSWER 1: _____

SECURITY ANSWER 2: _____

SECURITY ANSWER 3: _____

ADDITIONAL INFO: _____

_____

WEBSITE: _____

USER NAME: _____

PASSWORD: _____

SECURITY ANSWER 1: _____

SECURITY ANSWER 2: _____

SECURITY ANSWER 3: _____

ADDITIONAL INFO: _____

_____

****

WEBSITE: _____

USER NAME: _____

PASSWORD: _____

SECURITY ANSWER 1: _____

SECURITY ANSWER 2: _____

SECURITY ANSWER 3: _____

ADDITIONAL INFO: _____

_____

WEBSITE: _____

USER NAME: _____

PASSWORD: _____

SECURITY ANSWER 1: _____

SECURITY ANSWER 2: _____

SECURITY ANSWER 3: _____

ADDITIONAL INFO: _____

_____

****

WEBSITE: _____

USER NAME: _____

PASSWORD: _____

SECURITY ANSWER 1: _____

SECURITY ANSWER 2: _____

SECURITY ANSWER 3: _____

ADDITIONAL INFO: _____

_____

WEBSITE: _____

USER NAME: _____

PASSWORD: _____

SECURITY ANSWER 1: _____

SECURITY ANSWER 2: _____

SECURITY ANSWER 3: _____

ADDITIONAL INFO: _____

_____

****

WEBSITE: _____

USER NAME: _____

PASSWORD: _____

SECURITY ANSWER 1: _____

SECURITY ANSWER 2: _____

SECURITY ANSWER 3: _____

ADDITIONAL INFO: _____

_____

WEBSITE: _____

USER NAME: _____

PASSWORD: _____

SECURITY ANSWER 1: _____

SECURITY ANSWER 2: _____

SECURITY ANSWER 3: _____

ADDITIONAL INFO: _____

_____

****

WEBSITE: _____

USER NAME: _____

PASSWORD: _____

SECURITY ANSWER 1: _____

SECURITY ANSWER 2: _____

SECURITY ANSWER 3: _____

ADDITIONAL INFO: _____

_____

WEBSITE: _____

USER NAME: _____

PASSWORD: _____

SECURITY ANSWER 1: _____

SECURITY ANSWER 2: _____

SECURITY ANSWER 3: _____

ADDITIONAL INFO: _____

_____

****

WEBSITE: _____

USER NAME: _____

PASSWORD: _____

SECURITY ANSWER 1: _____

SECURITY ANSWER 2: _____

SECURITY ANSWER 3: _____

ADDITIONAL INFO: _____

_____

WEBSITE: _____

USER NAME: _____

PASSWORD: _____

SECURITY ANSWER 1: _____

SECURITY ANSWER 2: _____

SECURITY ANSWER 3: _____

ADDITIONAL INFO: _____

_____

****

WEBSITE: _____

USER NAME: _____

PASSWORD: _____

SECURITY ANSWER 1: _____

SECURITY ANSWER 2: _____

SECURITY ANSWER 3: _____

ADDITIONAL INFO: _____

_____

WEBSITE: _____

USER NAME: _____

PASSWORD: _____

SECURITY ANSWER 1: _____

SECURITY ANSWER 2: _____

SECURITY ANSWER 3: _____

ADDITIONAL INFO: _____

_____

****

WEBSITE: _____

USER NAME: _____

PASSWORD: _____

SECURITY ANSWER 1: _____

SECURITY ANSWER 2: _____

SECURITY ANSWER 3: _____

ADDITIONAL INFO: _____

_____

WEBSITE: _____

USER NAME: _____

PASSWORD: _____

SECURITY ANSWER 1: _____

SECURITY ANSWER 2: _____

SECURITY ANSWER 3: _____

ADDITIONAL INFO: _____

_____

****

WEBSITE: _____

USER NAME: _____

PASSWORD: _____

SECURITY ANSWER 1: _____

SECURITY ANSWER 2: _____

SECURITY ANSWER 3: _____

ADDITIONAL INFO: _____

_____

WEBSITE: _____

USER NAME: _____

PASSWORD: _____

SECURITY ANSWER 1: _____

SECURITY ANSWER 2: _____

SECURITY ANSWER 3: _____

ADDITIONAL INFO: _____

_____

****

WEBSITE: _____

USER NAME: _____

PASSWORD: _____

SECURITY ANSWER 1: _____

SECURITY ANSWER 2: _____

SECURITY ANSWER 3: _____

ADDITIONAL INFO: _____

_____

WEBSITE: _____

USER NAME: _____

PASSWORD: _____

SECURITY ANSWER 1: _____

SECURITY ANSWER 2: _____

SECURITY ANSWER 3: _____

ADDITIONAL INFO: _____

_____

****

WEBSITE: _____

USER NAME: _____

PASSWORD: _____

SECURITY ANSWER 1: _____

SECURITY ANSWER 2: _____

SECURITY ANSWER 3: _____

ADDITIONAL INFO: _____

_____

WEBSITE: _____

USER NAME: _____

PASSWORD: _____

SECURITY ANSWER 1: _____

SECURITY ANSWER 2: _____

SECURITY ANSWER 3: _____

ADDITIONAL INFO: _____

_____

****

WEBSITE: _____

USER NAME: _____

PASSWORD: _____

SECURITY ANSWER 1: _____

SECURITY ANSWER 2: _____

SECURITY ANSWER 3: _____

ADDITIONAL INFO: _____

_____

WEBSITE: _____

USER NAME: _____

PASSWORD: _____

SECURITY ANSWER 1: _____

SECURITY ANSWER 2: _____

SECURITY ANSWER 3: _____

ADDITIONAL INFO: _____

_____

****

WEBSITE: _____

USER NAME: _____

PASSWORD: _____

SECURITY ANSWER 1: _____

SECURITY ANSWER 2: _____

SECURITY ANSWER 3: _____

ADDITIONAL INFO: _____

_____

WEBSITE: _____

USER NAME: _____

PASSWORD: _____

SECURITY ANSWER 1: _____

SECURITY ANSWER 2: _____

SECURITY ANSWER 3: _____

ADDITIONAL INFO: _____

_____

****

WEBSITE: _____

USER NAME: _____

PASSWORD: _____

SECURITY ANSWER 1: _____

SECURITY ANSWER 2: _____

SECURITY ANSWER 3: _____

ADDITIONAL INFO: _____

_____

WEBSITE: _____

USER NAME: _____

PASSWORD: _____

SECURITY ANSWER 1: _____

SECURITY ANSWER 2: _____

SECURITY ANSWER 3: _____

ADDITIONAL INFO: _____

_____

****

WEBSITE: _____

USER NAME: _____

PASSWORD: _____

SECURITY ANSWER 1: _____

SECURITY ANSWER 2: _____

SECURITY ANSWER 3: _____

ADDITIONAL INFO: _____

_____

WEBSITE: _____

USER NAME: _____

PASSWORD: _____

SECURITY ANSWER 1: _____

SECURITY ANSWER 2: _____

SECURITY ANSWER 3: _____

ADDITIONAL INFO: _____

_____

****

WEBSITE: _____

USER NAME: _____

PASSWORD: _____

SECURITY ANSWER 1: _____

SECURITY ANSWER 2: _____

SECURITY ANSWER 3: _____

ADDITIONAL INFO: _____

_____

WEBSITE: _____

USER NAME: _____

PASSWORD: _____

SECURITY ANSWER 1: _____

SECURITY ANSWER 2: _____

SECURITY ANSWER 3: _____

ADDITIONAL INFO: _____

_____

****

WEBSITE: _____

USER NAME: _____

PASSWORD: _____

SECURITY ANSWER 1: _____

SECURITY ANSWER 2: _____

SECURITY ANSWER 3: _____

ADDITIONAL INFO: _____

_____

WEBSITE: _____

USER NAME: _____

PASSWORD: _____

SECURITY ANSWER 1: _____

SECURITY ANSWER 2: _____

SECURITY ANSWER 3: _____

ADDITIONAL INFO: _____

_____

****

WEBSITE: _____

USER NAME: _____

PASSWORD: _____

SECURITY ANSWER 1: _____

SECURITY ANSWER 2: _____

SECURITY ANSWER 3: _____

ADDITIONAL INFO: _____

_____

WEBSITE: _____

USER NAME: _____

PASSWORD: _____

SECURITY ANSWER 1: _____

SECURITY ANSWER 2: _____

SECURITY ANSWER 3: _____

ADDITIONAL INFO: _____

_____

****

WEBSITE: _____

USER NAME: _____

PASSWORD: _____

SECURITY ANSWER 1: _____

SECURITY ANSWER 2: _____

SECURITY ANSWER 3: _____

ADDITIONAL INFO: _____

_____

WEBSITE: _____

USER NAME: _____

PASSWORD: _____

SECURITY ANSWER 1: _____

SECURITY ANSWER 2: _____

SECURITY ANSWER 3: _____

ADDITIONAL INFO: _____

_____

****

WEBSITE: _____

USER NAME: _____

PASSWORD: _____

SECURITY ANSWER 1: _____

SECURITY ANSWER 2: _____

SECURITY ANSWER 3: _____

ADDITIONAL INFO: _____

_____

WEBSITE: _____

USER NAME: _____

PASSWORD: _____

SECURITY ANSWER 1: _____

SECURITY ANSWER 2: _____

SECURITY ANSWER 3: _____

ADDITIONAL INFO: _____

_____

****

WEBSITE: _____

USER NAME: _____

PASSWORD: _____

SECURITY ANSWER 1: _____

SECURITY ANSWER 2: _____

SECURITY ANSWER 3: _____

ADDITIONAL INFO: _____

_____

WEBSITE: _____

USER NAME: _____

PASSWORD: _____

SECURITY ANSWER 1: _____

SECURITY ANSWER 2: _____

SECURITY ANSWER 3: _____

ADDITIONAL INFO: _____

_____

****

WEBSITE: _____

USER NAME: _____

PASSWORD: _____

SECURITY ANSWER 1: _____

SECURITY ANSWER 2: _____

SECURITY ANSWER 3: _____

ADDITIONAL INFO: _____

_____

WEBSITE: _____

USER NAME: _____

PASSWORD: _____

SECURITY ANSWER 1: _____

SECURITY ANSWER 2: _____

SECURITY ANSWER 3: _____

ADDITIONAL INFO: _____

_____

****

WEBSITE: _____

USER NAME: _____

PASSWORD: _____

SECURITY ANSWER 1: _____

SECURITY ANSWER 2: _____

SECURITY ANSWER 3: _____

ADDITIONAL INFO: _____

_____

WEBSITE: _____

USER NAME: _____

PASSWORD: _____

SECURITY ANSWER 1: _____

SECURITY ANSWER 2: _____

SECURITY ANSWER 3: _____

ADDITIONAL INFO: _____

_____

****

WEBSITE: _____

USER NAME: _____

PASSWORD: _____

SECURITY ANSWER 1: _____

SECURITY ANSWER 2: _____

SECURITY ANSWER 3: _____

ADDITIONAL INFO: _____

_____

WEBSITE: _____

USER NAME: _____

PASSWORD: _____

SECURITY ANSWER 1: _____

SECURITY ANSWER 2: _____

SECURITY ANSWER 3: _____

ADDITIONAL INFO: _____

_____

****

WEBSITE: _____

USER NAME: _____

PASSWORD: _____

SECURITY ANSWER 1: _____

SECURITY ANSWER 2: _____

SECURITY ANSWER 3: _____

ADDITIONAL INFO: _____

_____

WEBSITE: _____

USER NAME: _____

PASSWORD: _____

SECURITY ANSWER 1: _____

SECURITY ANSWER 2: _____

SECURITY ANSWER 3: _____

ADDITIONAL INFO: _____

_____

****

WEBSITE: _____

USER NAME: _____

PASSWORD: _____

SECURITY ANSWER 1: _____

SECURITY ANSWER 2: _____

SECURITY ANSWER 3: _____

ADDITIONAL INFO: _____

_____

WEBSITE: _____

USER NAME: _____

PASSWORD: _____

SECURITY ANSWER 1: _____

SECURITY ANSWER 2: _____

SECURITY ANSWER 3: _____

ADDITIONAL INFO: _____

_____

****

WEBSITE: _____

USER NAME: _____

PASSWORD: _____

SECURITY ANSWER 1: _____

SECURITY ANSWER 2: _____

SECURITY ANSWER 3: _____

ADDITIONAL INFO: _____

_____

WEBSITE: _____

USER NAME: _____

PASSWORD: _____

SECURITY ANSWER 1: _____

SECURITY ANSWER 2: _____

SECURITY ANSWER 3: _____

ADDITIONAL INFO: _____

_____

****

WEBSITE: _____

USER NAME: _____

PASSWORD: _____

SECURITY ANSWER 1: _____

SECURITY ANSWER 2: _____

SECURITY ANSWER 3: _____

ADDITIONAL INFO: _____

_____

WEBSITE: _____

USER NAME: _____

PASSWORD: _____

SECURITY ANSWER 1: _____

SECURITY ANSWER 2: _____

SECURITY ANSWER 3: _____

ADDITIONAL INFO: _____

_____

****

WEBSITE: _____

USER NAME: _____

PASSWORD: _____

SECURITY ANSWER 1: _____

SECURITY ANSWER 2: _____

SECURITY ANSWER 3: _____

ADDITIONAL INFO: _____

_____

WEBSITE: _____

USER NAME: _____

PASSWORD: _____

SECURITY ANSWER 1: _____

SECURITY ANSWER 2: _____

SECURITY ANSWER 3: _____

ADDITIONAL INFO: _____

_____

****

WEBSITE: _____

USER NAME: _____

PASSWORD: _____

SECURITY ANSWER 1: _____

SECURITY ANSWER 2: _____

SECURITY ANSWER 3: _____

ADDITIONAL INFO: _____

_____

WEBSITE: _____

USER NAME: _____

PASSWORD: _____

SECURITY ANSWER 1: _____

SECURITY ANSWER 2: _____

SECURITY ANSWER 3: _____

ADDITIONAL INFO: _____

_____

****

WEBSITE: _____

USER NAME: _____

PASSWORD: _____

SECURITY ANSWER 1: _____

SECURITY ANSWER 2: _____

SECURITY ANSWER 3: _____

ADDITIONAL INFO: _____

_____

WEBSITE: _____

USER NAME: _____

PASSWORD: _____

SECURITY ANSWER 1: _____

SECURITY ANSWER 2: _____

SECURITY ANSWER 3: _____

ADDITIONAL INFO: _____

_____

****

WEBSITE: _____

USER NAME: _____

PASSWORD: _____

SECURITY ANSWER 1: _____

SECURITY ANSWER 2: _____

SECURITY ANSWER 3: _____

ADDITIONAL INFO: _____

_____

WEBSITE: _____

USER NAME: _____

PASSWORD: _____

SECURITY ANSWER 1: _____

SECURITY ANSWER 2: _____

SECURITY ANSWER 3: _____

ADDITIONAL INFO: _____

_____

****

WEBSITE: _____

USER NAME: _____

PASSWORD: _____

SECURITY ANSWER 1: _____

SECURITY ANSWER 2: _____

SECURITY ANSWER 3: _____

ADDITIONAL INFO: _____

_____

WEBSITE: _____

USER NAME: _____

PASSWORD: _____

SECURITY ANSWER 1: _____

SECURITY ANSWER 2: _____

SECURITY ANSWER 3: _____

ADDITIONAL INFO: _____

_____

****

WEBSITE: _____

USER NAME: _____

PASSWORD: _____

SECURITY ANSWER 1: _____

SECURITY ANSWER 2: _____

SECURITY ANSWER 3: _____

ADDITIONAL INFO: _____

_____

WEBSITE: _____

USER NAME: _____

PASSWORD: _____

SECURITY ANSWER 1: _____

SECURITY ANSWER 2: _____

SECURITY ANSWER 3: _____

ADDITIONAL INFO: _____

_____

****

WEBSITE: _____

USER NAME: _____

PASSWORD: _____

SECURITY ANSWER 1: _____

SECURITY ANSWER 2: _____

SECURITY ANSWER 3: _____

ADDITIONAL INFO: _____

_____

WEBSITE: _____

USER NAME: _____

PASSWORD: _____

SECURITY ANSWER 1: _____

SECURITY ANSWER 2: _____

SECURITY ANSWER 3: _____

ADDITIONAL INFO: _____

_____

****

WEBSITE: _____

USER NAME: _____

PASSWORD: _____

SECURITY ANSWER 1: _____

SECURITY ANSWER 2: _____

SECURITY ANSWER 3: _____

ADDITIONAL INFO: _____

_____

WEBSITE: _____

USER NAME: _____

PASSWORD: _____

SECURITY ANSWER 1: _____

SECURITY ANSWER 2: _____

SECURITY ANSWER 3: _____

ADDITIONAL INFO: _____

_____

****

WEBSITE: _____

USER NAME: _____

PASSWORD: _____

SECURITY ANSWER 1: _____

SECURITY ANSWER 2: _____

SECURITY ANSWER 3: _____

ADDITIONAL INFO: _____

_____

WEBSITE: _____

USER NAME: _____

PASSWORD: _____

SECURITY ANSWER 1: _____

SECURITY ANSWER 2: _____

SECURITY ANSWER 3: _____

ADDITIONAL INFO: _____

_____

****

WEBSITE: _____

USER NAME: _____

PASSWORD: _____

SECURITY ANSWER 1: _____

SECURITY ANSWER 2: _____

SECURITY ANSWER 3: _____

ADDITIONAL INFO: _____

_____

WEBSITE: _____

USER NAME: _____

PASSWORD: _____

SECURITY ANSWER 1: _____

SECURITY ANSWER 2: _____

SECURITY ANSWER 3: _____

ADDITIONAL INFO: _____

_____

****

WEBSITE: _____

USER NAME: _____

PASSWORD: _____

SECURITY ANSWER 1: _____

SECURITY ANSWER 2: _____

SECURITY ANSWER 3: _____

ADDITIONAL INFO: _____

_____

WEBSITE: _____

USER NAME: _____

PASSWORD: _____

SECURITY ANSWER 1: _____

SECURITY ANSWER 2: _____

SECURITY ANSWER 3: _____

ADDITIONAL INFO: _____

_____

****

WEBSITE: _____

USER NAME: _____

PASSWORD: _____

SECURITY ANSWER 1: _____

SECURITY ANSWER 2: _____

SECURITY ANSWER 3: _____

ADDITIONAL INFO: _____

_____

WEBSITE: _____

USER NAME: _____

PASSWORD: _____

SECURITY ANSWER 1: _____

SECURITY ANSWER 2: _____

SECURITY ANSWER 3: _____

ADDITIONAL INFO: _____

_____

****

WEBSITE: _____

USER NAME: _____

PASSWORD: _____

SECURITY ANSWER 1: _____

SECURITY ANSWER 2: _____

SECURITY ANSWER 3: _____

ADDITIONAL INFO: _____

_____

WEBSITE: _____

USER NAME: _____

PASSWORD: _____

SECURITY ANSWER 1: _____

SECURITY ANSWER 2: _____

SECURITY ANSWER 3: _____

ADDITIONAL INFO: _____

_____

****

WEBSITE: _____

USER NAME: _____

PASSWORD: _____

SECURITY ANSWER 1: _____

SECURITY ANSWER 2: _____

SECURITY ANSWER 3: _____

ADDITIONAL INFO: _____

_____

WEBSITE: _____

USER NAME: _____

PASSWORD: _____

SECURITY ANSWER 1: _____

SECURITY ANSWER 2: _____

SECURITY ANSWER 3: _____

ADDITIONAL INFO: _____

_____

****

WEBSITE: _____

USER NAME: _____

PASSWORD: _____

SECURITY ANSWER 1: _____

SECURITY ANSWER 2: _____

SECURITY ANSWER 3: _____

ADDITIONAL INFO: _____

_____

WEBSITE: _____

USER NAME: _____

PASSWORD: _____

SECURITY ANSWER 1: _____

SECURITY ANSWER 2: _____

SECURITY ANSWER 3: _____

ADDITIONAL INFO: _____

_____

****

WEBSITE: _____

USER NAME: _____

PASSWORD: _____

SECURITY ANSWER 1: _____

SECURITY ANSWER 2: _____

SECURITY ANSWER 3: _____

ADDITIONAL INFO: _____

_____

WEBSITE: _____

USER NAME: _____

PASSWORD: _____

SECURITY ANSWER 1: _____

SECURITY ANSWER 2: _____

SECURITY ANSWER 3: _____

ADDITIONAL INFO: _____

_____

****

WEBSITE: _____

USER NAME: _____

PASSWORD: _____

SECURITY ANSWER 1: _____

SECURITY ANSWER 2: _____

SECURITY ANSWER 3: _____

ADDITIONAL INFO: _____

_____

WEBSITE: _____

USER NAME: _____

PASSWORD: _____

SECURITY ANSWER 1: _____

SECURITY ANSWER 2: _____

SECURITY ANSWER 3: _____

ADDITIONAL INFO: _____

_____

****

WEBSITE: _____

USER NAME: _____

PASSWORD: _____

SECURITY ANSWER 1: _____

SECURITY ANSWER 2: _____

SECURITY ANSWER 3: _____

ADDITIONAL INFO: _____

_____

WEBSITE: _____

USER NAME: _____

PASSWORD: _____

SECURITY ANSWER 1: _____

SECURITY ANSWER 2: _____

SECURITY ANSWER 3: _____

ADDITIONAL INFO: _____

_____

****

WEBSITE: _____

USER NAME: _____

PASSWORD: _____

SECURITY ANSWER 1: _____

SECURITY ANSWER 2: _____

SECURITY ANSWER 3: _____

ADDITIONAL INFO: _____

_____

WEBSITE: _____

USER NAME: _____

PASSWORD: _____

SECURITY ANSWER 1: _____

SECURITY ANSWER 2: _____

SECURITY ANSWER 3: _____

ADDITIONAL INFO: _____

_____

****

WEBSITE: _____

USER NAME: _____

PASSWORD: _____

SECURITY ANSWER 1: _____

SECURITY ANSWER 2: _____

SECURITY ANSWER 3: _____

ADDITIONAL INFO: _____

_____

WEBSITE: _____

USER NAME: _____

PASSWORD: _____

SECURITY ANSWER 1: _____

SECURITY ANSWER 2: _____

SECURITY ANSWER 3: _____

ADDITIONAL INFO: _____

_____

****

WEBSITE: _____

USER NAME: _____

PASSWORD: _____

SECURITY ANSWER 1: _____

SECURITY ANSWER 2: _____

SECURITY ANSWER 3: _____

ADDITIONAL INFO: _____

_____

WEBSITE: _____

USER NAME: _____

PASSWORD: _____

SECURITY ANSWER 1: _____

SECURITY ANSWER 2: _____

SECURITY ANSWER 3: _____

ADDITIONAL INFO: _____

_____

****

WEBSITE: _____

USER NAME: _____

PASSWORD: _____

SECURITY ANSWER 1: _____

SECURITY ANSWER 2: _____

SECURITY ANSWER 3: _____

ADDITIONAL INFO: _____

_____

WEBSITE: _____

USER NAME: _____

PASSWORD: _____

SECURITY ANSWER 1: _____

SECURITY ANSWER 2: _____

SECURITY ANSWER 3: _____

ADDITIONAL INFO: _____

_____

****

WEBSITE: _____

USER NAME: _____

PASSWORD: _____

SECURITY ANSWER 1: _____

SECURITY ANSWER 2: _____

SECURITY ANSWER 3: _____

ADDITIONAL INFO: _____

_____

WEBSITE: _____

USER NAME: _____

PASSWORD: _____

SECURITY ANSWER 1: _____

SECURITY ANSWER 2: _____

SECURITY ANSWER 3: _____

ADDITIONAL INFO: _____

_____

****

WEBSITE: _____

USER NAME: _____

PASSWORD: _____

SECURITY ANSWER 1: _____

SECURITY ANSWER 2: _____

SECURITY ANSWER 3: _____

ADDITIONAL INFO: _____

_____

WEBSITE: _____

USER NAME: _____

PASSWORD: _____

SECURITY ANSWER 1: _____

SECURITY ANSWER 2: _____

SECURITY ANSWER 3: _____

ADDITIONAL INFO: _____

_____

****

WEBSITE: _____

USER NAME: _____

PASSWORD: _____

SECURITY ANSWER 1: _____

SECURITY ANSWER 2: _____

SECURITY ANSWER 3: _____

ADDITIONAL INFO: _____

_____

WEBSITE: _____

USER NAME: _____

PASSWORD: _____

SECURITY ANSWER 1: _____

SECURITY ANSWER 2: _____

SECURITY ANSWER 3: _____

ADDITIONAL INFO: _____

_____

****

WEBSITE: _____

USER NAME: _____

PASSWORD: _____

SECURITY ANSWER 1: _____

SECURITY ANSWER 2: _____

SECURITY ANSWER 3: _____

ADDITIONAL INFO: _____

_____

WEBSITE: _____

USER NAME: _____

PASSWORD: _____

SECURITY ANSWER 1: _____

SECURITY ANSWER 2: _____

SECURITY ANSWER 3: _____

ADDITIONAL INFO: _____

_____

****

WEBSITE: _____

USER NAME: _____

PASSWORD: _____

SECURITY ANSWER 1: _____

SECURITY ANSWER 2: _____

SECURITY ANSWER 3: _____

ADDITIONAL INFO: _____

_____

WEBSITE: _____

USER NAME: _____

PASSWORD: _____

SECURITY ANSWER 1:_____

SECURITY ANSWER 2:_____

SECURITY ANSWER 3:_____

ADDITIONAL INFO:_____

_____

****

WEBSITE: _____

USER NAME: _____

PASSWORD: _____

SECURITY ANSWER 1:_____

SECURITY ANSWER 2:_____

SECURITY ANSWER 3:_____

ADDITIONAL INFO:_____

_____

WEBSITE: _____

USER NAME: _____

PASSWORD: _____

SECURITY ANSWER 1: _____

SECURITY ANSWER 2: _____

SECURITY ANSWER 3: _____

ADDITIONAL INFO: _____

_____

****

WEBSITE: _____

USER NAME: _____

PASSWORD: _____

SECURITY ANSWER 1: _____

SECURITY ANSWER 2: _____

SECURITY ANSWER 3: _____

ADDITIONAL INFO: _____

_____

WEBSITE: _____

USER NAME: _____

PASSWORD: _____

SECURITY ANSWER 1: _____

SECURITY ANSWER 2: _____

SECURITY ANSWER 3: _____

ADDITIONAL INFO: _____

_____

****

WEBSITE: _____

USER NAME: _____

PASSWORD: _____

SECURITY ANSWER 1: _____

SECURITY ANSWER 2: _____

SECURITY ANSWER 3: _____

ADDITIONAL INFO: _____

_____

WEBSITE: _____

USER NAME: _____

PASSWORD: _____

SECURITY ANSWER 1: _____

SECURITY ANSWER 2: _____

SECURITY ANSWER 3: _____

ADDITIONAL INFO: _____

_____

****

WEBSITE: _____

USER NAME: _____

PASSWORD: _____

SECURITY ANSWER 1: _____

SECURITY ANSWER 2: _____

SECURITY ANSWER 3: _____

ADDITIONAL INFO: _____

_____

WEBSITE: _____

USER NAME: _____

PASSWORD: _____

SECURITY ANSWER 1:_____

SECURITY ANSWER 2:_____

SECURITY ANSWER 3:_____

ADDITIONAL INFO:_____

_____

****

WEBSITE: _____

USER NAME: _____

PASSWORD: _____

SECURITY ANSWER 1:_____

SECURITY ANSWER 2:_____

SECURITY ANSWER 3:_____

ADDITIONAL INFO:_____

_____

WEBSITE: _____

USER NAME: _____

PASSWORD: _____

SECURITY ANSWER 1: _____

SECURITY ANSWER 2: _____

SECURITY ANSWER 3: _____

ADDITIONAL INFO: _____

_____

****

WEBSITE: _____

USER NAME: _____

PASSWORD: _____

SECURITY ANSWER 1: _____

SECURITY ANSWER 2: _____

SECURITY ANSWER 3: _____

ADDITIONAL INFO: _____

_____

WEBSITE: _____

USER NAME: _____

PASSWORD: _____

SECURITY ANSWER 1: _____

SECURITY ANSWER 2: _____

SECURITY ANSWER 3: _____

ADDITIONAL INFO: _____

_____

****

WEBSITE: _____

USER NAME: _____

PASSWORD: _____

SECURITY ANSWER 1: _____

SECURITY ANSWER 2: _____

SECURITY ANSWER 3: _____

ADDITIONAL INFO: _____

_____

WEBSITE: _____

USER NAME: _____

PASSWORD: _____

SECURITY ANSWER 1: _____

SECURITY ANSWER 2: _____

SECURITY ANSWER 3: _____

ADDITIONAL INFO: _____

_____

****

WEBSITE: _____

USER NAME: _____

PASSWORD: _____

SECURITY ANSWER 1: _____

SECURITY ANSWER 2: _____

SECURITY ANSWER 3: _____

ADDITIONAL INFO: _____

_____

WEBSITE: _____

USER NAME: _____

PASSWORD: _____

SECURITY ANSWER 1: _____

SECURITY ANSWER 2: _____

SECURITY ANSWER 3: _____

ADDITIONAL INFO: _____

_____

****

WEBSITE: _____

USER NAME: _____

PASSWORD: _____

SECURITY ANSWER 1: _____

SECURITY ANSWER 2: _____

SECURITY ANSWER 3: _____

ADDITIONAL INFO: _____

_____

WEBSITE: _____

USER NAME: _____

PASSWORD: _____

SECURITY ANSWER 1: _____

SECURITY ANSWER 2: _____

SECURITY ANSWER 3: _____

ADDITIONAL INFO: _____

_____

****

WEBSITE: _____

USER NAME: _____

PASSWORD: _____

SECURITY ANSWER 1: _____

SECURITY ANSWER 2: _____

SECURITY ANSWER 3: _____

ADDITIONAL INFO: _____

_____

WEBSITE: _____

USER NAME: _____

PASSWORD: _____

SECURITY ANSWER 1: _____

SECURITY ANSWER 2: _____

SECURITY ANSWER 3: _____

ADDITIONAL INFO: _____

_____

****

WEBSITE: _____

USER NAME: _____

PASSWORD: _____

SECURITY ANSWER 1: _____

SECURITY ANSWER 2: _____

SECURITY ANSWER 3: _____

ADDITIONAL INFO: _____

_____

WEBSITE: _____

USER NAME: _____

PASSWORD: _____

SECURITY ANSWER 1: _____

SECURITY ANSWER 2: _____

SECURITY ANSWER 3: _____

ADDITIONAL INFO: _____

_____

****

WEBSITE: _____

USER NAME: _____

PASSWORD: _____

SECURITY ANSWER 1: _____

SECURITY ANSWER 2: _____

SECURITY ANSWER 3: _____

ADDITIONAL INFO: _____

_____

WEBSITE: _____

USER NAME: _____

PASSWORD: _____

SECURITY ANSWER 1: _____

SECURITY ANSWER 2: _____

SECURITY ANSWER 3: _____

ADDITIONAL INFO: _____

_____

****

WEBSITE: _____

USER NAME: _____

PASSWORD: _____

SECURITY ANSWER 1: _____

SECURITY ANSWER 2: _____

SECURITY ANSWER 3: _____

ADDITIONAL INFO: _____

_____

WEBSITE: _____

USER NAME: _____

PASSWORD: _____

SECURITY ANSWER 1: _____

SECURITY ANSWER 2: _____

SECURITY ANSWER 3: _____

ADDITIONAL INFO: _____

_____

****

WEBSITE: _____

USER NAME: _____

PASSWORD: _____

SECURITY ANSWER 1: _____

SECURITY ANSWER 2: _____

SECURITY ANSWER 3: _____

ADDITIONAL INFO: _____

_____

WEBSITE: _____

USER NAME: _____

PASSWORD: _____

SECURITY ANSWER 1: _____

SECURITY ANSWER 2: _____

SECURITY ANSWER 3: _____

ADDITIONAL INFO: _____

_____

****

WEBSITE: _____

USER NAME: _____

PASSWORD: _____

SECURITY ANSWER 1: _____

SECURITY ANSWER 2: _____

SECURITY ANSWER 3: _____

ADDITIONAL INFO: _____

_____

WEBSITE: _____

USER NAME: _____

PASSWORD: _____

SECURITY ANSWER 1: _____

SECURITY ANSWER 2: _____

SECURITY ANSWER 3: _____

ADDITIONAL INFO: _____

_____

****

WEBSITE: _____

USER NAME: _____

PASSWORD: _____

SECURITY ANSWER 1: _____

SECURITY ANSWER 2: _____

SECURITY ANSWER 3: _____

ADDITIONAL INFO: _____

_____

WEBSITE: _____

USER NAME: _____

PASSWORD: _____

SECURITY ANSWER 1: _____

SECURITY ANSWER 2: _____

SECURITY ANSWER 3: _____

ADDITIONAL INFO: _____

_____

****

WEBSITE: _____

USER NAME: _____

PASSWORD: _____

SECURITY ANSWER 1: _____

SECURITY ANSWER 2: _____

SECURITY ANSWER 3: _____

ADDITIONAL INFO: _____

_____

WEBSITE: _____

USER NAME: _____

PASSWORD: _____

SECURITY ANSWER 1: _____

SECURITY ANSWER 2: _____

SECURITY ANSWER 3: _____

ADDITIONAL INFO: _____

_____

****

WEBSITE: _____

USER NAME: _____

PASSWORD: _____

SECURITY ANSWER 1: _____

SECURITY ANSWER 2: _____

SECURITY ANSWER 3: _____

ADDITIONAL INFO: _____

_____

WEBSITE: _____

USER NAME: _____

PASSWORD: _____

SECURITY ANSWER 1: _____

SECURITY ANSWER 2: _____

SECURITY ANSWER 3: _____

ADDITIONAL INFO: _____

_____

****

WEBSITE: _____

USER NAME: _____

PASSWORD: _____

SECURITY ANSWER 1: _____

SECURITY ANSWER 2: _____

SECURITY ANSWER 3: _____

ADDITIONAL INFO: _____

_____

WEBSITE: _____

USER NAME: _____

PASSWORD: _____

SECURITY ANSWER 1: _____

SECURITY ANSWER 2: _____

SECURITY ANSWER 3: _____

ADDITIONAL INFO: _____

_____

****

WEBSITE: _____

USER NAME: _____

PASSWORD: _____

SECURITY ANSWER 1: _____

SECURITY ANSWER 2: _____

SECURITY ANSWER 3: _____

ADDITIONAL INFO: _____

_____

WEBSITE: _____

USER NAME: _____

PASSWORD: _____

SECURITY ANSWER 1: _____

SECURITY ANSWER 2: _____

SECURITY ANSWER 3: _____

ADDITIONAL INFO: _____

_____

****

WEBSITE: _____

USER NAME: _____

PASSWORD: _____

SECURITY ANSWER 1: _____

SECURITY ANSWER 2: _____

SECURITY ANSWER 3: _____

ADDITIONAL INFO: _____

_____

WEBSITE: _____

USER NAME: _____

PASSWORD: _____

SECURITY ANSWER 1: _____

SECURITY ANSWER 2: _____

SECURITY ANSWER 3: _____

ADDITIONAL INFO: _____

_____

****

WEBSITE: _____

USER NAME: _____

PASSWORD: _____

SECURITY ANSWER 1: _____

SECURITY ANSWER 2: _____

SECURITY ANSWER 3: _____

ADDITIONAL INFO: _____

_____

WEBSITE: _____

USER NAME: _____

PASSWORD: _____

SECURITY ANSWER 1: _____

SECURITY ANSWER 2: _____

SECURITY ANSWER 3: _____

ADDITIONAL INFO: _____

_____

****

WEBSITE: _____

USER NAME: _____

PASSWORD: _____

SECURITY ANSWER 1: _____

SECURITY ANSWER 2: _____

SECURITY ANSWER 3: _____

ADDITIONAL INFO: _____

_____

WEBSITE: _____

USER NAME: _____

PASSWORD: _____

SECURITY ANSWER 1: _____

SECURITY ANSWER 2: _____

SECURITY ANSWER 3: _____

ADDITIONAL INFO: _____

_____

****

WEBSITE: _____

USER NAME: _____

PASSWORD: _____

SECURITY ANSWER 1: _____

SECURITY ANSWER 2: _____

SECURITY ANSWER 3: _____

ADDITIONAL INFO: _____

_____

WEBSITE: _____

USER NAME: _____

PASSWORD: _____

SECURITY ANSWER 1: _____

SECURITY ANSWER 2: _____

SECURITY ANSWER 3: _____

ADDITIONAL INFO: _____

_____

****

WEBSITE: _____

USER NAME: _____

PASSWORD: _____

SECURITY ANSWER 1: _____

SECURITY ANSWER 2: _____

SECURITY ANSWER 3: _____

ADDITIONAL INFO: _____

_____

WEBSITE: _____

USER NAME: _____

PASSWORD: _____

SECURITY ANSWER 1: _____

SECURITY ANSWER 2: _____

SECURITY ANSWER 3: _____

ADDITIONAL INFO: _____

_____

****

WEBSITE: _____

USER NAME: _____

PASSWORD: _____

SECURITY ANSWER 1: _____

SECURITY ANSWER 2: _____

SECURITY ANSWER 3: _____

ADDITIONAL INFO: _____

_____

WEBSITE: _____

USER NAME: _____

PASSWORD: _____

SECURITY ANSWER 1: _____

SECURITY ANSWER 2: _____

SECURITY ANSWER 3: _____

ADDITIONAL INFO: _____

_____

****

WEBSITE: _____

USER NAME: _____

PASSWORD: _____

SECURITY ANSWER 1: _____

SECURITY ANSWER 2: _____

SECURITY ANSWER 3: _____

ADDITIONAL INFO: _____

_____

WEBSITE: _____

USER NAME: _____

PASSWORD: _____

SECURITY ANSWER 1: _____

SECURITY ANSWER 2: _____

SECURITY ANSWER 3: _____

ADDITIONAL INFO: _____

_____

****

WEBSITE: _____

USER NAME: _____

PASSWORD: _____

SECURITY ANSWER 1: _____

SECURITY ANSWER 2: _____

SECURITY ANSWER 3: _____

ADDITIONAL INFO: _____

_____

WEBSITE: _____

USER NAME: _____

PASSWORD: _____

SECURITY ANSWER 1: _____

SECURITY ANSWER 2: _____

SECURITY ANSWER 3: _____

ADDITIONAL INFO: _____

_____

****

WEBSITE: _____

USER NAME: _____

PASSWORD: _____

SECURITY ANSWER 1: _____

SECURITY ANSWER 2: _____

SECURITY ANSWER 3: _____

ADDITIONAL INFO: _____

_____

WEBSITE: _____

USER NAME: _____

PASSWORD: _____

SECURITY ANSWER 1: _____

SECURITY ANSWER 2: _____

SECURITY ANSWER 3: _____

ADDITIONAL INFO: _____

_____

****

WEBSITE: _____

USER NAME: _____

PASSWORD: _____

SECURITY ANSWER 1: _____

SECURITY ANSWER 2: _____

SECURITY ANSWER 3: _____

ADDITIONAL INFO: _____

_____

WEBSITE: _____

USER NAME: _____

PASSWORD: _____

SECURITY ANSWER 1: _____

SECURITY ANSWER 2: _____

SECURITY ANSWER 3: _____

ADDITIONAL INFO: _____

_____

****

WEBSITE: _____

USER NAME: _____

PASSWORD: _____

SECURITY ANSWER 1: _____

SECURITY ANSWER 2: _____

SECURITY ANSWER 3: _____

ADDITIONAL INFO: _____

_____

WEBSITE: _____

USER NAME: _____

PASSWORD: _____

SECURITY ANSWER 1: _____

SECURITY ANSWER 2: _____

SECURITY ANSWER 3: _____

ADDITIONAL INFO: _____

_____

****

WEBSITE: _____

USER NAME: _____

PASSWORD: _____

SECURITY ANSWER 1: _____

SECURITY ANSWER 2: _____

SECURITY ANSWER 3: _____

ADDITIONAL INFO: _____

_____

WEBSITE: _____

USER NAME: _____

PASSWORD: _____

SECURITY ANSWER 1: _____

SECURITY ANSWER 2: _____

SECURITY ANSWER 3: _____

ADDITIONAL INFO: _____

_____

****

WEBSITE: _____

USER NAME: _____

PASSWORD: _____

SECURITY ANSWER 1: _____

SECURITY ANSWER 2: _____

SECURITY ANSWER 3: _____

ADDITIONAL INFO: _____

_____

WEBSITE: _____

USER NAME: _____

PASSWORD: _____

SECURITY ANSWER 1: _____

SECURITY ANSWER 2: _____

SECURITY ANSWER 3: _____

ADDITIONAL INFO: _____

_____

****

WEBSITE: _____

USER NAME: _____

PASSWORD: _____

SECURITY ANSWER 1: _____

SECURITY ANSWER 2: _____

SECURITY ANSWER 3: _____

ADDITIONAL INFO: _____

_____

WEBSITE: _____

USER NAME: _____

PASSWORD: _____

SECURITY ANSWER 1: _____

SECURITY ANSWER 2: _____

SECURITY ANSWER 3: _____

ADDITIONAL INFO: _____

_____

****

WEBSITE: _____

USER NAME: _____

PASSWORD: _____

SECURITY ANSWER 1: _____

SECURITY ANSWER 2: _____

SECURITY ANSWER 3: _____

ADDITIONAL INFO: _____

_____

WEBSITE: _____

USER NAME: _____

PASSWORD: _____

SECURITY ANSWER 1: _____

SECURITY ANSWER 2: _____

SECURITY ANSWER 3: _____

ADDITIONAL INFO: _____

_____

****

WEBSITE: _____

USER NAME: _____

PASSWORD: _____

SECURITY ANSWER 1: _____

SECURITY ANSWER 2: _____

SECURITY ANSWER 3: _____

ADDITIONAL INFO: _____

_____

WEBSITE: _____

USER NAME: _____

PASSWORD: _____

SECURITY ANSWER 1: _____

SECURITY ANSWER 2: _____

SECURITY ANSWER 3: _____

ADDITIONAL INFO: _____

_____

****

WEBSITE: _____

USER NAME: _____

PASSWORD: _____

SECURITY ANSWER 1: _____

SECURITY ANSWER 2: _____

SECURITY ANSWER 3: _____

ADDITIONAL INFO: _____

_____

WEBSITE: _____

USER NAME: _____

PASSWORD: _____

SECURITY ANSWER 1: _____

SECURITY ANSWER 2: _____

SECURITY ANSWER 3: _____

ADDITIONAL INFO: _____

_____

****

WEBSITE: _____

USER NAME: _____

PASSWORD: _____

SECURITY ANSWER 1: _____

SECURITY ANSWER 2: _____

SECURITY ANSWER 3: _____

ADDITIONAL INFO: _____

_____

WEBSITE: _____

USER NAME: _____

PASSWORD: _____

SECURITY ANSWER 1: _____

SECURITY ANSWER 2: _____

SECURITY ANSWER 3: _____

ADDITIONAL INFO: _____

_____

****

WEBSITE: _____

USER NAME: _____

PASSWORD: _____

SECURITY ANSWER 1: _____

SECURITY ANSWER 2: _____

SECURITY ANSWER 3: _____

ADDITIONAL INFO: _____

_____

WEBSITE: _____

USER NAME: _____

PASSWORD: _____

SECURITY ANSWER 1: _____

SECURITY ANSWER 2: _____

SECURITY ANSWER 3: _____

ADDITIONAL INFO: _____

_____

****

WEBSITE: _____

USER NAME: _____

PASSWORD: _____

SECURITY ANSWER 1: _____

SECURITY ANSWER 2: _____

SECURITY ANSWER 3: _____

ADDITIONAL INFO: _____

_____

WEBSITE: _____

USER NAME: _____

PASSWORD: _____

SECURITY ANSWER 1: _____

SECURITY ANSWER 2: _____

SECURITY ANSWER 3: _____

ADDITIONAL INFO: _____

_____

****

WEBSITE: _____

USER NAME: _____

PASSWORD: _____

SECURITY ANSWER 1: _____

SECURITY ANSWER 2: _____

SECURITY ANSWER 3: _____

ADDITIONAL INFO: _____

_____

WEBSITE: _____

USER NAME: _____

PASSWORD: _____

SECURITY ANSWER 1: _____

SECURITY ANSWER 2: _____

SECURITY ANSWER 3: _____

ADDITIONAL INFO: _____

_____

****

WEBSITE: _____

USER NAME: _____

PASSWORD: _____

SECURITY ANSWER 1: _____

SECURITY ANSWER 2: _____

SECURITY ANSWER 3: _____

ADDITIONAL INFO: _____

_____

WEBSITE: _____

USER NAME: _____

PASSWORD: _____

SECURITY ANSWER 1: _____

SECURITY ANSWER 2: _____

SECURITY ANSWER 3: _____

ADDITIONAL INFO: _____

_____

****

WEBSITE: _____

USER NAME: _____

PASSWORD: _____

SECURITY ANSWER 1: _____

SECURITY ANSWER 2: _____

SECURITY ANSWER 3: _____

ADDITIONAL INFO: _____

_____

WEBSITE: _____

USER NAME: _____

PASSWORD: _____

SECURITY ANSWER 1: _____

SECURITY ANSWER 2: _____

SECURITY ANSWER 3: _____

ADDITIONAL INFO: _____

_____

****

WEBSITE: _____

USER NAME: _____

PASSWORD: _____

SECURITY ANSWER 1: _____

SECURITY ANSWER 2: _____

SECURITY ANSWER 3: _____

ADDITIONAL INFO: _____

_____

WEBSITE: _____

USER NAME: _____

PASSWORD: _____

SECURITY ANSWER 1: _____

SECURITY ANSWER 2: _____

SECURITY ANSWER 3: _____

ADDITIONAL INFO: _____

_____

****

WEBSITE: _____

USER NAME: _____

PASSWORD: _____

SECURITY ANSWER 1: _____

SECURITY ANSWER 2: _____

SECURITY ANSWER 3: _____

ADDITIONAL INFO: _____

_____

WEBSITE: _____

USER NAME: _____

PASSWORD: _____

SECURITY ANSWER 1: _____

SECURITY ANSWER 2: _____

SECURITY ANSWER 3: _____

ADDITIONAL INFO: _____

_____

****

WEBSITE: _____

USER NAME: _____

PASSWORD: _____

SECURITY ANSWER 1: _____

SECURITY ANSWER 2: _____

SECURITY ANSWER 3: _____

ADDITIONAL INFO: _____

_____

WEBSITE: _____

USER NAME: _____

PASSWORD: _____

SECURITY ANSWER 1: _____

SECURITY ANSWER 2: _____

SECURITY ANSWER 3: _____

ADDITIONAL INFO: _____

_____

****

WEBSITE: _____

USER NAME: _____

PASSWORD: _____

SECURITY ANSWER 1: _____

SECURITY ANSWER 2: _____

SECURITY ANSWER 3: _____

ADDITIONAL INFO: _____

_____

WEBSITE: _____

USER NAME: _____

PASSWORD: _____

SECURITY ANSWER 1: _____

SECURITY ANSWER 2: _____

SECURITY ANSWER 3: _____

ADDITIONAL INFO: _____

_____

****

WEBSITE: _____

USER NAME: _____

PASSWORD: _____

SECURITY ANSWER 1: _____

SECURITY ANSWER 2: _____

SECURITY ANSWER 3: _____

ADDITIONAL INFO: _____

_____

WEBSITE: _____

USER NAME: _____

PASSWORD: _____

SECURITY ANSWER 1: _____

SECURITY ANSWER 2: _____

SECURITY ANSWER 3: _____

ADDITIONAL INFO: _____

_____

****

WEBSITE: _____

USER NAME: _____

PASSWORD: _____

SECURITY ANSWER 1: _____

SECURITY ANSWER 2: _____

SECURITY ANSWER 3: _____

ADDITIONAL INFO: _____

_____

WEBSITE: _____

USER NAME: _____

PASSWORD: _____

SECURITY ANSWER 1: _____

SECURITY ANSWER 2: _____

SECURITY ANSWER 3: _____

ADDITIONAL INFO: _____

_____

****

WEBSITE: _____

USER NAME: _____

PASSWORD: _____

SECURITY ANSWER 1: _____

SECURITY ANSWER 2: _____

SECURITY ANSWER 3: _____

ADDITIONAL INFO: _____

_____

WEBSITE: _____

USER NAME: _____

PASSWORD: _____

SECURITY ANSWER 1: _____

SECURITY ANSWER 2: _____

SECURITY ANSWER 3: _____

ADDITIONAL INFO: _____

_____

****

WEBSITE: _____

USER NAME: _____

PASSWORD: _____

SECURITY ANSWER 1: _____

SECURITY ANSWER 2: _____

SECURITY ANSWER 3: _____

ADDITIONAL INFO: _____

_____

WEBSITE: _____

USER NAME: _____

PASSWORD: _____

SECURITY ANSWER 1: _____

SECURITY ANSWER 2: _____

SECURITY ANSWER 3: _____

ADDITIONAL INFO: _____

_____

****

WEBSITE: _____

USER NAME: _____

PASSWORD: _____

SECURITY ANSWER 1: _____

SECURITY ANSWER 2: _____

SECURITY ANSWER 3: _____

ADDITIONAL INFO: _____

_____

WEBSITE: _____

USER NAME: _____

PASSWORD: _____

SECURITY ANSWER 1: _____

SECURITY ANSWER 2: _____

SECURITY ANSWER 3: _____

ADDITIONAL INFO: _____

_____

****

WEBSITE: _____

USER NAME: _____

PASSWORD: _____

SECURITY ANSWER 1: _____

SECURITY ANSWER 2: _____

SECURITY ANSWER 3: _____

ADDITIONAL INFO: _____

_____

WEBSITE: _____

USER NAME: _____

PASSWORD: _____

SECURITY ANSWER 1: _____

SECURITY ANSWER 2: _____

SECURITY ANSWER 3: _____

ADDITIONAL INFO: _____

_____

****

WEBSITE: _____

USER NAME: _____

PASSWORD: _____

SECURITY ANSWER 1: _____

SECURITY ANSWER 2: _____

SECURITY ANSWER 3: _____

ADDITIONAL INFO: _____

_____

WEBSITE: _____

USER NAME: _____

PASSWORD: _____

SECURITY ANSWER 1: _____

SECURITY ANSWER 2: _____

SECURITY ANSWER 3: _____

ADDITIONAL INFO: _____

_____

****

WEBSITE: _____

USER NAME: _____

PASSWORD: _____

SECURITY ANSWER 1: _____

SECURITY ANSWER 2: _____

SECURITY ANSWER 3: _____

ADDITIONAL INFO: _____

_____

WEBSITE: _____

USER NAME: _____

PASSWORD: _____

SECURITY ANSWER 1: _____

SECURITY ANSWER 2: _____

SECURITY ANSWER 3: _____

ADDITIONAL INFO: _____

_____

****

WEBSITE: _____

USER NAME: _____

PASSWORD: _____

SECURITY ANSWER 1: _____

SECURITY ANSWER 2: _____

SECURITY ANSWER 3: _____

ADDITIONAL INFO: _____

_____

WEBSITE: _____

USER NAME: _____

PASSWORD: _____

SECURITY ANSWER 1: _____

SECURITY ANSWER 2: _____

SECURITY ANSWER 3: _____

ADDITIONAL INFO: _____

_____

****

WEBSITE: _____

USER NAME: _____

PASSWORD: _____

SECURITY ANSWER 1: _____

SECURITY ANSWER 2: _____

SECURITY ANSWER 3: _____

ADDITIONAL INFO: _____

_____

WEBSITE: _____

USER NAME: _____

PASSWORD: _____

SECURITY ANSWER 1: _____

SECURITY ANSWER 2: _____

SECURITY ANSWER 3: _____

ADDITIONAL INFO: _____

_____

****

WEBSITE: _____

USER NAME: _____

PASSWORD: _____

SECURITY ANSWER 1: _____

SECURITY ANSWER 2: _____

SECURITY ANSWER 3: _____

ADDITIONAL INFO: _____

_____

WEBSITE: _____

USER NAME: _____

PASSWORD: _____

SECURITY ANSWER 1: _____

SECURITY ANSWER 2: _____

SECURITY ANSWER 3: _____

ADDITIONAL INFO: _____

_____

****

WEBSITE: _____

USER NAME: _____

PASSWORD: _____

SECURITY ANSWER 1: _____

SECURITY ANSWER 2: _____

SECURITY ANSWER 3: _____

ADDITIONAL INFO: _____

_____

WEBSITE: _____

USER NAME: _____

PASSWORD: _____

SECURITY ANSWER 1:_____

SECURITY ANSWER 2:_____

SECURITY ANSWER 3:_____

ADDITIONAL INFO:_____

_____

****

WEBSITE: _____

USER NAME: _____

PASSWORD: _____

SECURITY ANSWER 1:_____

SECURITY ANSWER 2:_____

SECURITY ANSWER 3:_____

ADDITIONAL INFO:_____

_____

WEBSITE: _____

USER NAME: _____

PASSWORD: _____

SECURITY ANSWER 1: _____

SECURITY ANSWER 2: _____

SECURITY ANSWER 3: _____

ADDITIONAL INFO: _____

_____

****

WEBSITE: _____

USER NAME: _____

PASSWORD: _____

SECURITY ANSWER 1: _____

SECURITY ANSWER 2: _____

SECURITY ANSWER 3: _____

ADDITIONAL INFO: _____

_____

WEBSITE: _____

USER NAME: _____

PASSWORD: _____

SECURITY ANSWER 1: _____

SECURITY ANSWER 2: _____

SECURITY ANSWER 3: _____

ADDITIONAL INFO: _____

_____

****

WEBSITE: _____

USER NAME: _____

PASSWORD: _____

SECURITY ANSWER 1: _____

SECURITY ANSWER 2: _____

SECURITY ANSWER 3: _____

ADDITIONAL INFO: _____

_____

WEBSITE: _____

USER NAME: _____

PASSWORD: _____

SECURITY ANSWER 1: _____

SECURITY ANSWER 2: _____

SECURITY ANSWER 3: _____

ADDITIONAL INFO: _____

_____

****

WEBSITE: _____

USER NAME: _____

PASSWORD: _____

SECURITY ANSWER 1: _____

SECURITY ANSWER 2: _____

SECURITY ANSWER 3: _____

ADDITIONAL INFO: _____

_____

www.ingramcontent.com/pod-product-compliance
Lightning Source LLC
Chambersburg PA
CBHW071002050326
40689CB00014B/3463